New Cousins

How to Trace
Living Descendants
of your Ancestors

Karen Bali

THE FAMILY HISTORY PARTNERSHIP

Published by
The Family History Partnership
57 Bury New Road
Ramsbottom, Bury
Lancashire BL0 0BZ

www.thefamilyhistorypartnership.com

ISBN: 978 1 906280 36 9

First published 2009
second edition 2012

Printed and bound by Berforts Information Press
Southfield Road, Eynsham, Oxford OX29 4JB

Contents

Introduction   4
   What is descendant searching?   4

PART ONE

Records, Sources and methods   5
   The General Register Office   5
   How can GRO records help living relatives?   8
   Census Records   9
   How can Census records help find living relatives?   11
   Wills   12
   How can Probate records help find living relatives?   12
   Electoral Registers   13
   How can Electoral Registers help find living relatives?   15
   Street and telephone directories   15
   How can directories help find living relatives?   16
   Local Newspapers   17
   How can newspapers help find living relatives?   18
   The Internet, including message board sites   19
   Family History Societies   21
   Getting Professional Help   22
   Putting it all together — how information from records
      can help you to trace living relatives   23

PART TWO

Making Contact   24
   Method of Contact   24
   Internet approaches   26
   When contact has been made   26
   DNA Testing   27
   Relationship chart: How are we related?   28
   Arranging a visit   29

Further Reading   31

Introduction

What is descendant searching?

Descendant searching is a different way to conduct family research, which is growing in popularity as resources in recent years have made it possible to look for living relatives. It can be fascinating, rewarding and potentially life-changing. Research leads you not to dead ancestors but living, breathing relatives who share your genetic heritage – members of your extended family.

Descendant searching involves using many of the same research methods as traditional family history research to bring a search forward in time rather than working backward chronologically. Working from a chosen ancestor or family, a researcher can trace living descendants from the same family and link up to share information.

New Cousins mainly covers records and resources for England and Wales but touches on those for other parts of the UK and overseas.

This guide assumes that the reader has some familiarity with basic family history resources and access to the internet. In addition to practical assistance with researching records, *New Cousins* also offers guidance on making an approach to your relatives when contact details have been identified.

With the help of this guide you could soon be exchanging letters, e-mails and phone calls with your distant cousins, and maybe even planning a visit. Readers are welcome to contact me with their success stories, to give feedback, use the free links on my web site or to request help with their research via my website at **www.people-search.co.uk**.

Karen Bali, 2012

PART ONE

Records, sources and methods

The General Register Office

Records of births, marriages and deaths have long been a valuable resource for family history researchers. Just as indexes and certificates are used to trace family lines back, they can also be used to trace forward.

GRO Indexes

From 1837 to the end of 1983 there is one alphabetical index for each year quarter. The inclusion of the mother's maiden name in indexes from mid 1911 helps to identify possible children from a marriage – this is most useful when tracing lines forward (see the example on page 7).

From 1984 indexes are compiled annually. The availability of searchable indexes via the Internet has been a great help to family history researchers in recent years. Copies of indexes, and digital images of index pages, can be searched and viewed on several websites (see below).

Free BMD has an excellent search engine, at **www.freebmd.org.uk**, which is an ongoing volunteer project to transcribe the indexes of births, marriages and deaths for England and Wales from 1837 to the present day. It is not yet complete and is most useful for nineteenth and early twentieth century research. When you find a possible entry for the event you are seeking you can find out more by clicking on the district name to tell you more about the district where the event was registered, and where the original registers might now be found. Also, by clicking the link on the page number, you can see other entries on the same page. This is most useful when looking at marriage records to check for possible spouses.

Ancestry is a subscription site **www.ancestry.co.uk** that also has comprehensive coverage of births, marriages and deaths plus many other records. **www.findmypast.com** is a comprehensive, pay per view site. Personally I find indexes on this site are the most accurate. You will need to subscribe or register and buy credits, but minimum fees are reasonable.

Not finding the entry?

Occasionally the index entry for a particular event will be missing, even though the event took place and is recorded in local registers. Omissions and mistranscriptions do occur, but usually the explanation is simpler.

Check under every possible spelling – names were often spelled phonetically and recorded as the registrar or official thought they sounded. Take dropped "aitches" and differences in vowel sounds into account.

It is possible that the event you are seeking is not indexed within the same quarter or year – it is the date of the registration, not the date of the actual event, which determines in which volume the index entry appears.

Birth entries might be missing or difficult to find for one of the following reasons:

- A certain amount of time, currently 42 days, is allowed for parents to register the birth of their baby. It is conceivable then that the birth might be registered in the following quarter or year.
- There was no penalty for non-registration of births until the 1870s. It is estimated that between 6% and 10% of births were not registered in earlier years of civil registration.
- Once a penalty was introduced, late registrations may have been recorded with an incorrect date of birth to avoid paying a fine.
- The parents may not have been married at the time of the birth; therefore the child would be recorded with the mother's maiden surname even if the mother and father later married each other.
- An illegitimate child might have later taken the surname of his or her step-father.
- If born after 1926, the child may have been adopted
- The birth may have taken place in a different district or county to the one where the family lived, because the mother was staying with relatives, for example.
- The child may have been born outside England and Wales – overseas and armed services indexes can be searched at the The National
- Archives and online at **www.findmypast.com**.
  The child may have been registered at birth with one forename but used another throughout life.
- If the parents were undecided about the name, or the child was not expected to live, the birth may have been originally recorded as simply 'male' or 'female'.

Death entries may also be missing because:

- The death may be recorded in a subsequent quarter because there was a delay in registration. If there was an inquest or complication it is possible for a death to be registered a year or more after the event.

- The person who registered the death was not aware of the correct name or age of the deceased. Usually a close relative will register a death but sometimes deaths were registered by a local official, acquaintance or health care professional.
- The name recorded at death is not the same as that recorded at birth or marriage because the deceased was generally known by another name.
- The death may have taken place outside England and Wales.
- War deaths are unlikely to be included in main indexes – overseas and armed services indexes are in separate indexes, which are available on **www.findmypast.com** or, more informatively for the two World Wars, on the Commonwealth War Graves Commission debt of honour register at **www.cwgc.org**.
- The age recorded may be incorrect because the person who registered the death did not know exactly how old the deceased was.

Marriage entries may be missing because:
- The marriage took place earlier or later than the researcher expected. Parents may not have been married before the birth of the first child or married many years before having a surviving child.
- The marriage did not take place at all. Despite the misconception that living together is a modern phenomenon, couples often set up home together without being married.
- The names may not have been recorded as expected at the time of the marriage. Even if previous or subsequent records show one name, the order of forenames or spellings might have been recorded differently at the time of the marriage.
- The marriage did not take place in England and Wales. Look for clues, including places of birth on census entries, indicating that the family came from abroad or elsewhere in the British Isles. Young couples sometimes eloped to Scotland if their families disapproved of the marriage.

When a promising index entry is found, a copy of the certificate will give more details about the event and family members. Ways that certificates can be obtained from the General Register office can be found by selecting 'Order Certificates' at **www.gro.gov.uk**. Alternatively, certificates can often be ordered from the Register Office in the district where the event took place. Policy varies – some offices will accept orders by telephone, others insist on a written application. A few districts will not issue certificates for family history research and many will not search for a marriage within their registers unless the exact date and place of marriage is known. The home page of the GRO has a 'Search for your local register office' facility, and an alphabetical list can be found on Genuki at **www.ukbmd.org.uk/genuki/reg/regoff.html**

Note: It may be difficult for you to order the birth certificate of any relative who was born less than 50 years ago because of General Register Office anti-fraud measures. Requesting a copy of the certificate by post from the local register office for the district where the birth was registered, together with a detailed explanation of your connection and supporting documents may overcome this.

Alternatively, genealogists who are members of AGRA **www.agra.org.uk** have approval to order recent birth certificates and may be willing to obtain one on your behalf. Read more about certificates and the services of the GRO at **www.direct.gov.uk/en/Governmentcitizensandrights/**

Registeringlifeevents/index.htm

How can GRO records help find living relatives?

Example: Certificates tell us so much about individuals and families that it is possible to use this resource alone to trace relatives. For example, if your great-grandfather was Frank Alfred Edwards born 1916 in Kent it should be easy to locate his birth record and obtain a copy of the full certificate. This will tell you the names of both his parents and the maiden name of his mother. From this you will be able to locate their marriage record giving their ages at the time, which may prove useful if you need to identify their death records. To identify Frank's brothers and sisters use the 'mother's maiden name' column in birth indexes. This was introduced into indexes from the third quarter of 1911 and is invaluable when seeking to identify children from a marriage. If the surname, district and mother's maiden name all match up you almost certainly have children of the same couple. Use indexes to find marriage records for Frank's brothers and sisters – the most recent certificate will tell you whether or not their father was deceased at the time. Birth records for Frank's nieces and nephews will move the search into a generation that might possibly be living, or maybe recently deceased. The death certificate for any member of the family will give you the name and address of the informant – the relative who registered the death, usually a member of the immediate family.

This method works well provided the family followed the usual social rules of marriage before children and children born within a marriage.

If you have any problems finding birth records for your relatives try looking for children who may have been born before the marriage under the mother's maiden name. If no birth record is found where one is expected you might also try the indexes of adopted children (arranged alphabetically in annual volumes from 1927 onwards) that, along with birth marriage and death indexes, are held at selected repositories throughout England and Wales, including:

- Manchester City Library
  www.manchester.gov.uk/info/448/archives_and_local_studies
- Birmingham Central Library
  www.birmingham.gov.uk/centrallibrary
- Bridgend Reference and Information Library
  **www.bridgend.gov.uk/web/groups/public/documents/
  services/001666.hcs**
- Plmouth Central Library **www.plymouth.gov.uk/libraries**
- City of Westminster Archives Centre
  www.westminster.gov.uk/services/libraries/archives
- The British Library, London* **www.bl.uk**

Census Records

Leaping from decade to decade it is sometimes possible to track ancestors forward fifty years in less than hour using searchable census indexes, transcriptions and digital images on the internet.

Census data is only released after 100 years - at present, the 1911 census is the latest full census available. Almost all census returns for England and Wales between 1841 and 1911 have been transcribed and indexed and are searchable online. Digital images of the original returns are also widely available.

However, the indexes are not always accurate. There are sometimes errors in the spelling and interpretation of names, occupations and places of birth. It may take several attempts, searching by first name and age or surname and county, to link one family with another on a subsequent census.

www.ancestry.co.uk has a comprehensive collection of census data and images but the most accurate indexes tend to be those compiled by family history societies, many of which can be found at **www.findmypast.com**. There are links to various census data sites and products, such as CD ROM's at **www.sandn.net/ukcensus.htm**.

The wealth of information that census returns contain can, in some cases, lead to relatives who may have died quite recently, and whose children may still be living. It is also possible to track families through each decade, finding perhaps three or four generations to add to your family tree.

Census returns are also available on microfilm or microfiche at repositories throughout England and Wales, and in many libraries worldwide. Family history

---

* Visitors to the British Library will need to register for membership, which requires two forms of identification (with a current address) to be produced.

societies often produce surname indexes for their county. Many have a dedicated team of volunteers who work hard to index and transcribe their records, including census returns.

Census returns can also usually be viewed at Church of Jesus Christ of Latter Day Saints' Family History Centres – find your nearest branch at **www.familysearch.org/Eng/Library/FHC/frameset_fhc.asp**

Census returns are available to search and view on the following Internet sites – some sites charge for viewing transcriptions or digital images:

www.ancestry.co.uk
www.findmypast.com
www.freecen.org.uk
www.1901censusonline.com
www.familysearch.org
www.ukcensusonline.com

Not finding your relative?
If you have searched for your ancestors online using census records without success, consider the following:

- The name may be spelled phonetically – with many illiterate working class residents and no standardisation of spelling, sometimes names were spelled as they sounded. Try saying the name aloud and noting all possible spellings then do separate searches on all of these.
- The age of your ancestor may not be accurate – some people guessed how old they were and some (especially women) pretended to be younger. Also, the age of children was sometimes recorded as higher than the actual age because parents were sending those who were underage out to work. In 1841 the exact age was only recorded if the occupant was under 18, otherwise it was rounded down to the nearest multiple of 5.
- A name may have been changed from a previous census return or certificate for a number of reasons – females may have remarried or children may have taken the name of a stepfather. Foreign names were often 'anglicised' either by officials or by the family in order to fit in with the community.
- Your ancestor may have been away from home on census night. Relatives who were travelling, visiting, working away from home or on a shipping vessel would have been recorded at the place where they stayed and not at their usual address.
- Some surnames were changed due to terms of inheritance in the will of a wealthy (often childless) relative who wanted his or her surname to survive.

- Entries are sometimes transcribed incorrectly – try searching with a 'soundex' feature if available, or searching just by first name, age and place of birth. You may find, however, that some strange (and seemingly unrelated) spellings results with the soundex feature.

Tip Soundex is an American system which links similar surnames (such as Hayward, Heyward, Heywood etc). It is used in the International Genealogical Index (IGI). For more information see **www.archives.gov/genealogy/census/soundex.html**

How can Census records help find living relatives?

Example: Let us say that your ancestor was Francis Watkins, who married in 1878. His marriage certificates states that he was age 24 at the time, his occupation was recorded as 'carpenter' he lived in Surrey and his father was William Watkins, lamp lighter (deceased). 'Emily Watkins' was a witness.

A search of the 1871 census online might locate Francis aged 17 in a Surrey household with his occupation recorded as 'apprentice carpenter'. It is also recorded that his place of birth was 'Epsom, Surrey'. In the household with Francis were other members of his family

- *His father, William, (who was still living at this time) aged 46 who was born in London and whose occupation was 'lamp lighter'*
- *His mother, Emily (then aged 40), of no occupation and born in Cardiff*
- *His sister Sarah, aged 19, who was a seamstress and who was also born in Epsom*
- *His young brother Walter aged 8 who is recorded as a 'scholar', and was born in Woking, Surrey*

With just one document you have established considerable information not only about Francis but also about his family and background.

Moving forward to the 1881 census you may find that his mother was recorded as a widow working as a wood cutter, his sister Sarah had left the household and that his brother Walter was by then working as a lamp lighter, the same occupation as his late father.

You can continue to track Walter forward to find out if he married and had children. You may find that Emily appears in a later census return as an elderly widow with her married daughter, son-in-law and grandchildren.

So the census can tell you not just about your ancestor's past, but about his or her family and their later lives.

Wills

Probate records are among the most useful, but often overlooked sources in family history research. They not only provide details of a person's property and possessions, but also valuable information about their family, particularly the names and addresses beneficiaries of their estate who usually survived them.

In England and Wales from the fourteenth century to 1858, probate was granted by church courts. The most important court was the Prerogative Court of Canterbury, whose records are at The National Archives and are fully indexed at **www.nationalarchives.gov.uk/documentsonline**. The system is explained at **www.nationalarchives.gov.uk/catalogue/RdLeaflet.asp?sLeafletID=220&j=1**

In 1858 the Court of Probate was created and the responsibility for proving wills transferred from the churches to this civil department.

Probate now falls under the jurisdiction of the Family Division of the Court Service. Indexes and copies of wills from 1858 are available from the Principal Registry of the Family Division, First Avenue House, Holborn (or any district probate registry), but applications must be made in person. Same day collection is no longer available at First Avenue House. Find out more at **www.justice.gov.uk/courts/probate/copies-of-grants-wills**.

Postal requests for copies of wills (the current cost for a four year search, including a copy of the will or grant of probate is currently £6) can be made to the Probate Registry in Leeds by completing a PA1S application form (available from the courts service web site, above). However, postal applications can take up to four weeks. Apply to:

The Postal Searches and Copies Department
Leeds District Probate Registry
York House
York Place
Leeds
LS1 2BA

Microfiche copies of indexes from 1858 to 1943 are held at many libraries and record offices in the UK including The National Archives.

How can Probate records help find living relatives?

Example: Your ancestor was Georgina Willson born 1878 in Northumberland. It is known that her father was George Willson, a tailor who owned two shops and several properties. George's will made in 1915 and proved in 1919, names not only his wife, Rosina Ruby Willson, but also his other children – Sidney William Willson who inherited his businesses and Fanny Greene, wife of Albert Greene, solicitor, who inherited one of his properties.

The will of Rosina Ruby Willson may tell you more about her children and grandchildren at the time of her death and might include addresses of her executors and beneficiaries.

For Information about wills in Wales, read web page on probate records by The National Library of Wales **www.llgc.org.uk/index.php?id=487** - they hold Welsh probates up to 1858 and copies of wills after from 1858 to 1940.

Electoral Registers

These are an often overlooked resource that can sometimes reveal valuable information about the family who were resident in a particular household.

Also known as voters' lists, these are registers of people who are eligible to vote in households within a parliamentary constituency.

Traditionally arranged geographically by parliamentary ward and street, these registers could, until recently, be searched only by address. Now that computers have converted the registers into formats which can be alphabetically indexed, searching of recent editions by name is possible (see below).

Early electoral registers will of course only feature men, but it was only in 1885 that most men gained the vote – all men over 21 and women over 30 who were householders could vote from 1918. This was lowered to the age of 21 to match the age at which men could vote in 1928. The voting age for all adults was lowered to 18 in 1970.

The survival and availability of historical electoral registers varies considerably between different areas. They are often found in local studies libraries and sometimes archives offices Some local authorities have an almost complete set of registers dating back to before 1900 – others just a handful of registers from recent decades.

Policies of access vary considerably, as local government officers interpret laws on data protection in different ways. Some authorities have an 'open access' policy and are happy to look up entries for households in response to enquiries by telephone, letter or email. Others are more cautious – some officials may take it upon themselves to interpret the law strictly. They may not only refuse to give information from current registers to members of the public, but also unilaterally impose the removal of former registers (for up to 50 years) from archives and library shelves.

Some authorities will do short searches for free but many have introduced charged research, which can vary from £10 to £35 per hour. Where there is no research service, a list of local researchers can usually be supplied by the repository.

The British Library has a large collection of historical electoral registers, but you will need a reader's pass to use them – details can be found at **www.bl.uk/reshelp/findhelprestype/offpubs/electreg/electoral.html**.

Read '*Electoral Registers 1832-1948 and Burgess Rolls*' by Jeremy Gibson (2008) for more detailed information about historical electoral registers.

Electoral registers online

A recent development has been the availability of electoral registers in a searchable format, available on the Internet. The first searchable registers were made available on CD-ROM to the public in the mid 1990s and were a revelation; anyone in the UK could be found using these discs or databases and researchers were saved hours of trawling through volumes at local libraries.

Unfortunately, researchers were not the only ones using these resources; companies used them to compile mailing and telephone lists, others used them to find relatives and lost loves who did not wish to be found. There was considerable anger and indignation as people became aware that this information, collected by local authorities as a statutory requirement, was being sold to absolutely anyone.

Consequently, voters now have the right to request that their details are not sold or made available in registers for public consultation, rather like having an unlisted phone number. Although this rule has been in place just a few years, already around a quarter of the electorate have opted out of the public register and details of their address are not made available.

One of the latest and most comprehensive versions of the electoral registers online is provided by Tracesmart at **www.tracesmart.co.uk** Tracesmart is a company that started as an investigation service tracing people who owed money. You will need to register and pay to search and view the results but minimum charges for private users are reasonable.

Not only does Tracesmart provide a search facility for the electoral register but you can also reverse search by address to find out who lives there. There is even a facility to search for couples or members of the same family by combining names to narrow down the matches. The results for a person search will give you not only their address, but also the names of everyone else registered at that address and any listed telephone number. There is an option to obtain the names of neighbours and even the facility to order property ownership records. Tracesmart supplements the electoral register database with data from other sources – the Tracesmart register. This is a collection of privately gathered data that has been compiled into one large database to fill in gaps and provide addresses for some who might otherwise not be traceable.

Another online electoral register and telephone directory search service is 192 at www.192.com. In addition it offers birth, marriage and death indexes, the

1861 census, and an excellent mapping service which allows you to get aerial views of individual houses. It is free to search but you need to register and purchase units to view the results of your searches, except free directory enquiries. 192 also currently charges a one-off fee for viewing results from all but the latest electoral registers.

Ancestry **www.ancestry.co.uk** is undertaking a project to provide online digital images of electoral registers for England and Wales. The first phase has already been released. You can search them by clicking on the Search Tab from the home page and selecting Census and Electoral Rolls. Read more about the release of London registers at **http://blogs.ancestry.com/uk/2012/01/11/ 130-years-of-london-electoral-registers-released-today/**

How can Electoral Registers help find living relatives?

Example: Say you have letters from a relative with the surname Brent who lived in Dorset in the 1960s. The person who wrote most of them is long deceased but she talks of her grandson, Edwin (her son's only child) tells of his graduation and news of his career. In 1965 she describes Edwin's marriage to a girl called Tina in the local church and a year later the birth of their first son, Alistair George. Historical electoral registers might identify Edwin and Tina at the same address for a number of years, being joined later by Edwin's widowed mother and their children as they reach voting age. A search of online electoral registers may find Edwin and Tina still together at an address in the same area if you are lucky. If they are no longer together, one or both are deceased or they have retired abroad, you might still find their son, the baby Alistair, probably now a father himself. With two forenames (if he enters them both on electoral registration form as required, although only the first name and middle initial are displayed) he will be distinguishable from other entries for Alistair Brent.

Street and telephone directories

Street directories were a popular part of our communities for almost two centuries. Telephone directories, once in everyday use, are now less comprehensive. However, using a combination of these two resources can be helpful in local research.

Street directories not only contained lists of residents, but also details about the county, town or parish where they lived, together with information about local trades and services. Many different companies produced these directories and more than 350 were published in England and Wales during the 1930s. After the war there was a gradual decline because of high production costs and competition from telephone directories. Kelly's dominated the market for a number of years, but the last street directories were published in the mid-1970s. Early street directories may only contain 'notable' residents of a town or village – the doctor, postmaster, lawyer etc – and wealthy property owners. Toward the mid-1900s, many urban directories listed all householders. However, only one name per property is listed – this would have been the person considered to be 'the head of the household' (usually the man but women were often listed if they were widows, spinsters or property owners). Also, only adults were listed – no children were included in these directories.

Directories are usually found in the local studies library or archives office in the area that they covered – www.familia.org.uk will tell you who has what.

Increasingly, old directories are sold or made available in electronic format. Particularly useful is www.historicaldirectories.org which offers free access to digitised images. They are also readily available on CD from genealogy companies including S&N (**www.genealogysupplies.com**), Stepping Stones (**www.stepping-stones.co.uk**) and Your Old Books and Maps (**http://youroldbooksandmaps.co.uk**)

How can directories help find living relatives?

Example: Your ancestor, David Atkins, was born in Southampton in 1919. His father was Alfred Atkins, a tailor. Searching street directories for the area where they lived you discover that Alfred had a shop and that he was listed in street directories as the proprietor until 1937. After World War Two, the shop remained but was then called 'A Atkins & Son' with G Atkins listed as the proprietor and 'A Atkins' a resident in a nearby street. A Atkins disappears from the street directory after 1954 so it might be assumed that he was living until this time (although sometimes entries can appear in directories for two or three years after someone has died). G Atkins continues to be listed in street directories until 1971 when another person takes over his shop, but an entry under George Atkins in the 1972 street directory finds him resident in the same street where his father lived. A search of telephone directories shows G Atkins listed at that address until 1989, with a J Atkins continuing to be listed until the present day. A letter or call to 'J Atkins' finds the elderly widow of George Atkins, who is able to provide details of the Atkins family history and also put you in touch with relatives of her late husband.

Telephone directories
The public telephone service was introduced in 1879 and the first telephone directory was published the following year. It was not until well into the 1950s and 1960s, however, that household telephones became popular and directories

became widely used. From the 1950s, when more ordinary householders subscribed to a telephone service, to the mid-1980s, almost everyone with a telephone was listed in the directory covering the area where they lived.

Usually the titled, the very rich or those with sensitive professions such as policemen and politicians had unlisted (ex-directory) numbers. Although anyone could have an unlisted phone number it was not free so few ordinary people did.

Once companies discovered how to use directories to sell to householders, however, the percentage of ex-directory numbers increased by the year in an attempt to stop unsolicited sales calls. From 5 per cent of unlisted numbers in 1975, the total has increased to around 75 per cent.

Entries in telephone directories give only the surname, initials, address and telephone number of the subscriber – usually the person who pays the bill. Historical directories are often kept in local libraries for the area that they cover but an almost complete set of directories for the whole of the UK from the late 1800s is kept at British Telecom Archives in London **www.btplc.com/Thegroup/BTsHistory/BTgrouparchives**. They do not offer a research service and access to the collection is in person by appointment only. Digitised images and a comprehensive name index for historical telephone directories between 1880 and 1984 are also available online at **www.ancestry.co.uk.**

There are several searchable online sources for current telephone directories, the official version is provided by BT at **www.thephonebook.bt.com** Infobel world links to directories not only in the UK but also worldwide - **www.infobel.com/world**.

Local newspapers

Historically local newspapers published notices of births, marriages and deaths, and often reports on christenings, weddings and funerals. These usually mention the names of other family members who were present at events.

Local studies libraries and archives offices usually hold these newspapers on microfilm.

Alternatively, most newspapers can currently be found at:

British Library Newspapers Collection
Colindale Avenue
London NW9 5HE
Tel 020 7412 7353

This library has a searchable online catalogue so that you can check holdings before you visit. The British Library plans to close the Colindale Newspapers Library in 2012. Hard copies of papers are gradually being removed to the Boston Spa site for digitisation. Check the web site for latest information **www.bl.uk** or telephone 020 7412 7353.

Read 'Local Newspapers, 1750-1920' by Jeremy Gibson (2002) for more information about newspaper holdings in England and Wales.

How can newspapers help find living relatives?

Example: *Your great grandfather's brother was Geoffrey Nelson from Dorset. He died at the age of 46 in 1922 and was survived by his wife Winfred, who registered his death. Geoffrey and Winifred had two daughters but their married names are not known and Winifred's sister registered her death 19 years later. However, the report of Winifred's funeral in the local newspaper is very detailed and contains lots of information about the family. It reads:*

...Mrs Nelson's elder daughter, Mrs Caroline Toogood from Chichester led the mourners and she was accompanied by her son Michael. The younger daughter of Mrs Nelson, Mrs Evelyn Collier, was unable to attend because she has a newborn baby and lives in Somerset, where her husband is working at present. ..

So within this short paragraph you have the married names and places of residence of both daughters, and also the name of one of her grand-children.

Today, many local newspapers have a regular section where they feature appeals for missing relatives. Some papers also have an online version where readers can search archives and submit appeals.

There are a number of resources to help you find the newspaper that covers the area where a family you are seeking comes from, or is thought to be living.

Willings Press Guide lists information about and contact details for publications in the UK, including all local and regional newspapers. You can search by the name of the paper or geographically by the county, town, region or city that it covers.

A reference copy of *Willings Press Guide* can be found in many public libraries and second hand issues can often be purchased on ebay **www.ebay.co.uk.**

Another way to find contact details for local newspapers is to search online.

You could try entering likely terms such as 'Salisbury local newspaper' – Google's top result is the *Salisbury Journal*. There are also alphabetical lists of local newspapers - www.onlinenewspapers.com is quite comprehensive. The list includes:

- England A-K
- England L-Z
- Scotland
- Wales

There is a separate site for Ireland.

The Internet, including message board sites

The following are all useful websites that may help you to find living relatives:

Ancestry **www.ancestry.com** and **www.ancestry.co.uk**
A subscription service offering access to a vast amount of British and worldwide information and records. Ancestry offers a free trial and the membership fees for full access to the UK and Ireland Collection are payable either monthly or annually (currently around £110 a year). The extent is so wide and the quality and value of the records so high that this is undoubtedly worth the subscription fee. There is also a pay-per-view option for those who do not wish to commit to long term membership.

Family Search **www.familysearch.com** may hold useful information in Ancestral Files, IGI entries and Pedigree Resource Files where the name of a contributor may be recorded, often together with contact details. Sometimes addresses may be out of date but it may be possible to make contact or find more information through the contributor's nearest LDS Family History Centre. Addresses for these centres can be found on the FamilySearch website.

Genes Reunited **www.genesreunited.co.uk**
Genes Reunited is a huge success and has quickly become one of Britain's largest family and ancestry site with over 11 million users and 750 million individual names listed. The premise is simple – everyone who registers enters details about their relatives and ancestors and can link up with those who share the same ancestors. There is also a name search and email contact facility between members. It is easy to use, free to search and free to register but you will need to pay a nominal fee to send messages to possible relatives.

Guild of one-name studies **www.one-name.org**
This is an umbrella organisation for surname groups and studies. There is a searchable register that can link with those who may be researching the same surname or family line.

Metacrawler **www.metacrawler.com**
This site could help you to find relatives anywhere in the world. The powerful search facility can spot names on almost any of the millions of websites available on the Internet and show extracts in the form of listed results. It is best to use the double inverted commas in order to locate results where the first name and surname appear together e.g. *"Karen Bali"*. Although not helpful if you are looking for someone called Emma Ward or Paul Johnson, if your relative has a slightly unusual name or is connected with a particular profession or hobby – e.g. *Dentist "Jean Petworth"* – chances are high that Metacrawler will find them.

Missing You **www.missing-you.net**
A free message board site that offers an instant online posting services designed to help locate missing relatives, lost friends, former colleagues etc who are thought to be anywhere in the UK

Online English Names Directory **www.list.jaunay.com/engnames**
This is a searchable database of surnames submitted by individuals who are researching them. Not all counties are covered but there are links to the individual county surname sites not included in the main database.

Curious Fox **www.curiousfox.com**
The village by village contact site for anybody researching family history, genealogy and local history in the UK and Ireland. Every UK county, town and village has a page for family history, local history, surname and genealogy enquiries.

Origins Network **www.originsnetwork.com** from the Society of Genealogists provides online access to historical and family records from the whole of the British Isles dating back to the 13th century. Registration is required and fees are payable to search and view.

Rootsweb **www.rootsweb.com**
Rootsweb claims to be 'the oldest and largest free genealogy website'. It is certainly extensive with millions of names on their vast databases. It has a powerful site search facility, message boards for surnames, regions, religions and much more plus almost thirty thousand mailing lists – well worth checking out but make a large packed lunch and flask of tea before you start!

Cousin Connect **www.cousinconnect.com**
Cousin Connect was created to allow researchers to publish online queries and

designed to offer the best chance of connecting with relatives through its Query Notification Service and CousinConnect Network.

Facebook **www.facebook.com**

It is impossible to ignore the phenomenon that is Facebook as a means of connecting with others on the internet. At the end of 2011 Facebook had over 500 million members worldwide and over half of them log in every day. There are more than 23 Facebook members in the UK alone, well over one third of the population. The Family Tree app **www.facebook.com/familytree**, introduced in 2007, is proving very popular as a means of identifying family relationships and linking with relatives. Searching for a person by name, particularly if the name is popular, can be complicated. To narrow down searches, Facebook offers the following advice:

1. Type in the name of a friend in the search bar
2. Click the **See more results...** link at the bottom of the dropdown
3. Click **People** from the **Search Filters** menu on the right
4. Use the filter dropdown menu to filter your search results by location, education, or workplace, or add another filter option (e.g.: searching for your hometown will show you all of the people who have that town listed on their account as well)

Family History Societies

If you know the geographical area where your ancestor came from and if the family was settled, it is a good idea to join the family history society for the county where they lived. This may not only save you money on research but might also lead you directly to relatives. There is a family history society in each county in England and Wales and membership fees are usually very reasonable. The societies are run by volunteers with a passion for family history, many of whom who have extensive knowledge of county families. Members have access to local resources – indexes, transcripts, original documents etc and many societies offer a free or subsidised lookup service for members.

Lists of local surnames that members are researching or have researched are regularly published by societies or listed on their website so that those with the same ancestors can link up.

Letters and queries from members worldwide can be published in the society journals, which are usually published quarterly. An enquiry may take a few months to appear in a journal but you may quickly be contacted by members who are either connected with the family or can offer help with information, searches or location photographs. Read more about family history societies on the Federation of Family History Societies website at **www.ffhs.org.uk**. This web site also has links to local societies throughout the country.

Getting professional help

Sometimes it may be necessary to request a little help from researchers who are able to access original records not available online or in your area. Many genealogists advertise their services on the internet and in family history magazines but quality and reliability may vary. Some researchers have made this their profession – they are likely to be experienced and accurate but probably more expensive. Others offer research or 'lookup' services at lower cost – this for them may be a part-time hobby that provides interest and makes pocket money.

A good researcher in the area where your ancestor lived can be a valuable asset – he or she may not only be able to access original records, but also bring a wealth of local knowledge to your research, saving a great deal of time and effort:

AGRA

The Association of Genealogists and Researchers in Archives (formerly the Association of Genealogists and Record Agents), the oldest professional association for genealogical researchers in Britain. Formed in 1968, it maintains the highest standards of entry. Members must not only complete a lengthy application form but submit detailed examples of their research work, supply references and usually also attend an interview before being admitted to membership. Once admitted, members must adhere to a code of practice and risk the complaints procedure if their clients are not satisfied. Therefore, you should expect high standards of research and a professional approach from any AGRA member. AGRA members can be contacted via the association's website at **www.agra.org.uk.**

APG

The Association of Professional Genealogists (APG or Apgen) was founded in the USA but is fast becoming an International organisation with a reputation for professionalism. Experienced researchers can become members by submitting a CV and are expected to follow a code of conduct. Unlike AGRA, however, there is no application or examination procedure and no references are sought. Members of Apgen can be found in many parts of the world. Their website, at **www.apgen.org** is fully searchable, making it easy to find a researcher to suit your needs.

Web portals for researchers worldwide

www.expertgenealogy.com and **www.genealogypro.com** are sites where genealogists and family researchers can advertise their services. These sites are searchable by country and give a description of the service that individual researchers can offer. More experienced researchers tend to advertise their services on these sites and although no guarantee of quality can be given, the fact that the researcher has paid a fee to be listed should indicate that research is a profession rather than a hobby. Enquiries about services and fees can be made via these sites.

The Salvation Army
The Family Tracing Service of the Salvation Army is a valuable, subsidised public service, founded for the purpose of reunion between family members. Although they will not assist with research purely for the purpose of family history, they will help to find relatives within your extended family – cousins, aunts, uncles etc with whom you have lost touch, or with whom you may never have had personal contact. The advantage of this organisation is that it operates worldwide and can look for relatives outside the country where you live. A fee is payable for this service, but it is very reasonable and in many cases does not cover the true cost of the search. Visit **www.salvationarmy.org.uk/uki/ FamilyTracing** for more information.

Putting it all together – how information from records can help you trace living relatives

Starting with your original information, descendant searching is a case of linking information that connects your ancestor to a living relative. This is a little like a game of 'stepping stones', leaping forward chronologically from one record to another until you reach the current generation. You might start with the marriage certificate of your ancestor and using the information it contains, find a record of his or her birth. You should then be able to identify the family on a census return and work forward through the decades until the last available census. Noting ages of family members at this time, a search for marriages or deaths of individuals in the household may bring your search forward another decade or two. A search of street directories, using a local researcher to help you, may find that the family remained listed until the 1950s – death and probate records can identify the next generation and where they were living. Historical electoral registers can help you discover how long they remained at an address and who else was listed as resident with them – individuals disappear indicating that they may have died and children appear when they reach voting age. Online registers and telephone directories can lead you to your distant cousin.

This may sound easy, and sometimes it is, particularly if a family remained in the same town or has an uncommon surname. Often, however, it can take months of searching, making enquiries, reaching dead ends and receiving negative responses before you are finally able to make contact with a living relative.

PART TWO

Making contact

Once you have contact details for your relative, what then? You may get only one chance to link up with relatives, so it is important to get it right. Contact by telephone should be avoided as an initial approach unless you have no other contact information.

Contact by Letter

It is usually best to make your initial approach in writing by post, enclosing an s.a.e. to encourage the person you contact to respond. It is important when making contact by letter to take time gathering and sending the correct information, and above all getting across to your relative that the reason for your approach is genuine.

Whilst family history has become a very popular interest in this country in recent years, sadly, there are some who are indifferent to genetic links and the heritage of their family. Hopefully your research will lead to relatives with whom you can share your interest, but it is possible that the reaction of your relative to an approach from you explaining your connection will be 'So what?' or even worse 'Get lost'. Sometimes people can be sceptical, cynical or even hostile when approached by someone unknown to them. One of the reasons for this may be the huge number of attempts at contact in order to sell something, often disguised as an approach for another reason. It should also be pointed out that identity theft has grown rapidly as a method of fraud in order to steal from the accounts of innocent individuals or couples. Therefore, requests for personal information, particularly about names and dates of birth, may be viewed with suspicion. Try to make questions general and do not request specific dates of birth and marriage or their mother's maiden name, as this information is often used as bank security questions.

Also, try to avoid the 'I already know all about you' approach. Even though many records giving personal information exist, people from the older generation in particular may be unnerved by the fact that someone can find out information about them without their knowledge or consent.

Many people can be rather reserved about overt affection and anything that might be considered 'forward' including flowery, familiar language.

When the author questioned twenty people she knew at random to ask what they would do if they were contacted by a distant relative, the opinion was split:

Nine people said that they would be pleased, even excited, and that they would make contact immediately to find out more.

Five people said that they would only be slightly interested but would respond and be prepared to answer questions. Two of the five said they would be indifferent to the fact that the letter was from a distant relative.

Six people said that they would be suspicious and would not respond. Two used the word 'horrified' at the thought of relatives turning up on their doorstep.

The right things to say
Here is an example of a letter that is full of information, and makes no demands:

Dear Mr Coxley

My great-grandfather, George Coxley, born in Nether Walton, Hertforshire, in 1880 had an older brother, James Coxley.

In 1907 George married Alicia Greezley, (copy of marriage certificate enclosed), and their first son was my grandfather Derek Coxley (1909 – 1987). My mother Diane is Derek's middle daughter.

We know from census and other public reords that James married and had children, including one called Phillip born 1896 in Nether Walton. With the help of a researcher I have learned that you may be a descendant of Phillip Coxley. If so, I would be very happy to hear from you and to share with you the information I have gathered about the Coxley family in Hereford.

I have enclosed details of how to contact me, a copy of my draft family tree showing how I think we may be related, and some postage stamps should you wish to write.

If by any chance I have the wrong Robert Coxley, I am sorry to have troubled you. A short note, email or quick call to let me know would be much appreciated. I have enclosed a self-addressed envelope and first class stamp for your use.

With best wishes,

Daphne Girley (Mrs)

Speculative letters

Even if you are not certain whether the person you are writing to does have a connection, speculative letters – to all people with the same surname in the right area for example – can sometimes bring quick results. A batch of twenty letters can cost less than a few hours of research plus several photocopies. Even with speculative letters, taking the trouble to explain your research, print out a chart and enclose document copies may help to encourage a positive response from anyone with a connection.

What to enclose

First of all, a copy of a chart, hand drawn or computer generated, showing how you think that your two families are connected, is most important.

Copies of census returns and certificates that you have acquired during the course of your research could also be included, but not birth certificates relating to the person you are writing to or a member of their immediate family. Indicate clearly on each document what the information relates to e.g. *The 1891 census of Nether Walton showing the Coxley family living at 9 Crealey Cottages.*

If you wish, you could also include one or two copies of photographs, perhaps one of an ancestor and one of yourself – some people feel that it encourages a response if the person has a picture of the person they are writing to.

It is also a nice gesture to enclose a self-addressed envelope and per-haps postage stamps help toward the reply cost. The royal mail website at **www.royalmail.com** contains information about addressing envelopes correctly, a search facility for postcodes and an online shop for purchasing postage stamps.

Internet approaches

If you have found your relative via the internet, you may have only an email address or social network profile and perhaps no indication of the area in which he or she lives. If the email address was found on a site connected with family history you are half way there - this shows that your relative already has an interest and may be eager to respond. However, emails and internet messages should be clear, concise enquiries that give the receiver enough information but does not overload or ask too many questions.

When contact has been made

Exchanging information

Once you have successfully established contact with your relative you can begin to discover more about their family, exchange information and slowly get to know one another. Do take it slowly though – don't bombard them with requests for information or pester if they are not quite as quick to reply as you would like. Working out how you are related to each other is a nice way to break the ice and having a 'third cousin once removed' may be a novelty that your relative is proud to tell everyone about.

Charts like this can help you to work out the name of the relationship between two members within the same extended family. There are other charts and relationship calculators on the following web sites:

www.rhodesfamily.org.uk/people/relationship.html
www.searchforancestors.com/utility/cousincalculator.html

DNA testing

A fascinating recent development in the field of family research, DNA testing can not only provide scientific insight into your ancient genetic roots, but also potentially prove a link between individuals going back many generations.

Every one of us inherits genetic material from our parents that remains unchanged through the generations - some of the genes can determine ancient ancestors or prove connections to recent ancestor. The main type of genetic test that is of interest to those researching their family history is for Y chromosome (male) DNA. This tests for DNA that is passed from father to son and remains unchanged through generations, proving genetic links.

There are other types of DNA test that do not usually help with family history research. Mitochondrial (female) and autosomal (race percentage) tests are offered by a number of companies but the results, particularly for race DNA, can be vague or conflicting.

Detailed explanations of the science behind these tests and how they can help your research can be found on these sites, together with information about the cost and procedure:

www.oxfordancestors.com

Professor Bryan Sykes, the founder of Oxford Ancestors, has written two interesting and very readable books, one about female DNA called 'The Seven Daughters of Eve' and another about male genetics called 'Adam's Curse: A future without men'. Oxford Ancestors is a laboratory service for genealogy related DNA testing.

www.dnaandfamilyhistory.com

This is a website to complement a book of the same name, 'DNA And Family History' by Chris Pomery. It contains much information about male and female DNA, free downloads and an online order facility for the book and DNA testing kits. The book is now out of print but a new book, by the same author, was

How are we related?

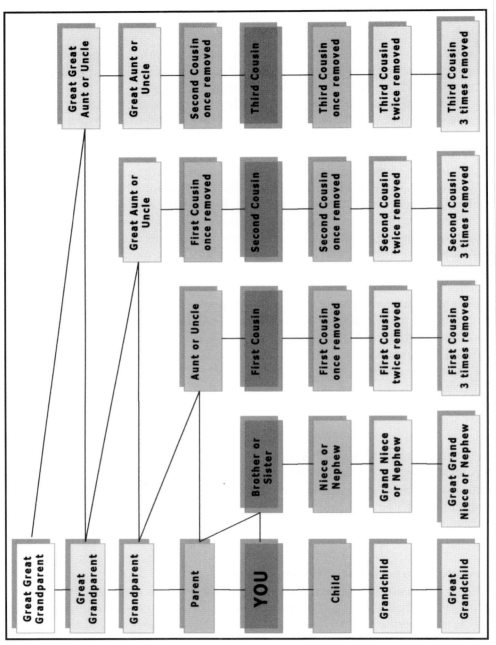

published in 2007: 'Family History in the Genes: Trace Your DNA and Grow Your Family Tree' (National Archives).

www.familytreedna.com
Claiming to be the oldest DNA company specifically for genealogy, Family Tree DNA has over 32,000 records of DNA markers that can be matched with others from all over the world.

www.dnaheritage.com
This company has offices in the UK and USA and claims to test every sample twice to ensure accuracy.

www.genetree.com
Genetree offers male and female DNA tests and an online community web site where members can share information.

Important Note
Approach DNA testing with **extreme** caution as it may reveal hitherto unsuspected illegitimacy and cause enormous upset. Unless the newly-discovered relatives live in a different county, DNA testing should not be suggested until after a meeting, and preferably not until the parties have met a number of times.

Arranging a visit
The time may come when correspondence or conversation with your new-found relative turns to plans to meet in person. It is best if this is raised or suggested by them, but if you would like to plan a visit or had been considering it anyway, approach the subject slowly. Rather than saying 'we would like to visit you' or 'we are coming to meet you', it may be better (after at least a month or two from your first contact) to say that you would like to see the home town of your ancestor and visit sites connected with your family. Ask if they can suggest where to stay (make it clear that you don't expect to stay with them) and places to visit (houses, churches, libraries etc). When arrangements are made, and if your relative has not already suggested it, ask if it is possible to meet with them in person. Be sure to take as much information as you are able about your shared family tree and a good camera, preferably digital, not just for snaps of the family, but buildings, historical documents and even gravestones.

Plan an itinerary before you leave to make the most of your visit and ensure that nothing is missed. If further research is part of your plan for the visit, check details and opening times for libraries and archives and have a clear objective of what you want to achieve.

If your relative does not live near the old family home it is best to plan the first meeting on neutral ground, perhaps nearer his or her home to make it easier. You could suggest meeting up for a meal or in a public venue that has a café or restaurant. Meet Half Way www.meethalfway.com has a tool for calculating a meeting point that is half way between two destinations.

Keeping in touch
The Internet is the quickest, cheapest and most convenient way to keep in touch with relatives. Apart from email messages, photographs and documents can be scanned, saved and sent as email attachments.

Gedcom can be exchanged to keep family tree information up to date and saves typing out and sending lots of information. In case you are not familiar with Gedcom, it is an abbreviation for a standard format used for transmitting and transferring genealogical data from one computer and genealogy program to another. It was developed by the Church of Jesus Christ of Latter Day Saints and a detailed explanation with downloadable Gedcom programmes can be found on their website:

**www.familysearch.org/Eng/Home/FAQ/
frameset_faq.asp?FAQ=faq_gedcom.asp**

My Family at **www.myfamily.com** is a cost-effective way of developing a private family website that also serves as a forum to exchange news, post messages and keep in touch with relatives no matter how much your family is scattered across the globe. There is a free basic package, and a more comprehensive 'Essentials' package, which costs around £25 a year, which when shared between just a few relatives can save much more when you consider the usual cost of keeping in touch with postage stamps, stationery, cards and phone calls.

Further Reading

How To Plan Family Reunions
Quick Easy Guides, 2008

Christian, Peter
The Genealogist's Internet
The National Archives, 2009

Genealogy Online for Dummies - UK Edition
John Wiley & Sons, 2006

Pomery, Chris
Family History in the Genes: Trace Your DNA and Grow Your Family Tree
The National Archives, 2007

Raymond, Stuart A
Netting Your Ancestors
Family History Partnership, 2007

Bali, Karen
The People Finder: Reuniting Relatives, Finding Friends
Nicholas Brealey, 2007

Recommended:
Karen recommends Pharos Teaching and Tutoring – online courses for family history research:
www.pharostutors.com

Please visit the People Search website for information and up to date links to help you find people:
www.people-search.co.uk

See our wide range of family history titles at

www.thefamilyhistorypartnership.com